Why We Eat Fruits

by Beth Bence Reinke, MS, RD

BUMBA BOOKS™

Note to Educators:

Throughout this book, you'll find critical thinking questions. These can be used to engage young readers in thinking critically about the topic and in using the text and photos to do so.

Lerner Publications Company
A division of Lerner Publishing Group, Inc.
241 First Avenue North
Minneapolis, MN 55401 USA

For reading levels and more information, look up this title at www.lernerbooks.com.

Library of Congress Cataloging-in-Publication Data

Names: Reinke, Beth Bence, author.
Title: Why we eat fruits / Beth Bence Reinke, MS, RD.
Description: Minneapolis : Lerner Publications, [2018] | Series: Bumba books. Nutrition matters | Audience: Ages 4–7. | Audience: K to grade 3. | Includes bibliographical references and index.
Identifiers: LCCN 2017047422 (print) | LCCN 2017057859 (ebook) | ISBN 9781541507692 (eb pdf) | ISBN 9781541503359 (lb : alk. paper) | ISBN 9781541526839 (pb : alk. paper)
Subjects: LCSH: Fruit in human nutrition—Juvenile literature. | Fruit—Juvenile literature. | Nutrition—Juvenile literature.
Classification: LCC QP144.F78 (ebook) | LCC QP144.F78 R45 2018 (print) | DDC 613.2/8—dc23

LC record available at https://lccn.loc.gov/2017047422

Manufactured in the United States of America
1 – CG – 7/15/18

Table of
Contents

All about Fruit

Fruits give your

body energy.

You need energy to

play and grow.

Did you eat fruit today?

There is juice in fruit.

The juice is mostly water.

Eating fruit gives your

body water.

Why do you think your body needs water?

Fruits have fiber.

Fiber makes your stomach feel full.

It helps you digest.

Lots of fruits have vitamin C.

Vitamin C makes your gums

and skin strong.

It helps cuts heal.

Potassium is a mineral in many fruits.

It helps your heart pump blood.

Potassium helps your muscles

work too.

Why do you think your body needs different vitamins and minerals?

Your body needs vitamin C and

potassium every day.

Eat fruit at meals.

Or eat it as a snack.

Fruits are colorful.

Different colored fruits help your body

in different ways.

Eating a rainbow of fruit colors is

good for you.

What kinds of colorful fruit do you eat?

You need three servings of fruit each day.

Peel a banana. Munch on grapes.

Chomp a crunchy apple!

19

Eating fruit helps you

grow up healthy.

What are your

favorite fruits?

USDA MyPlate Diagram

This much of your plate should be filled with fruit.

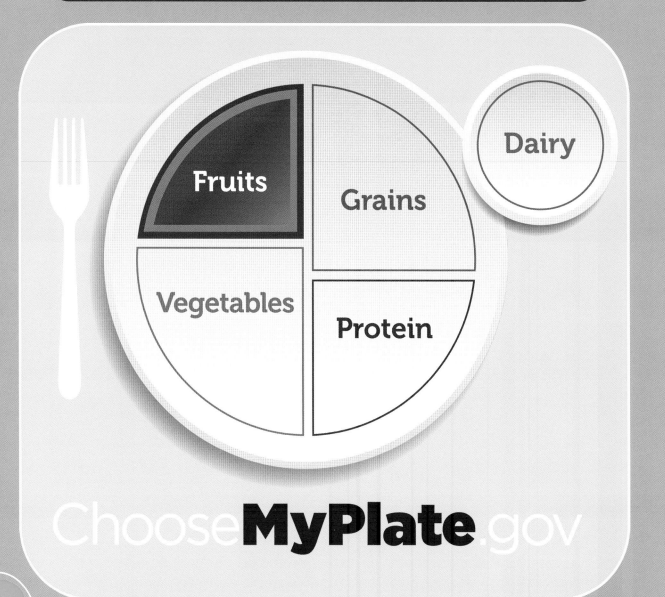

Picture Glossary

digest

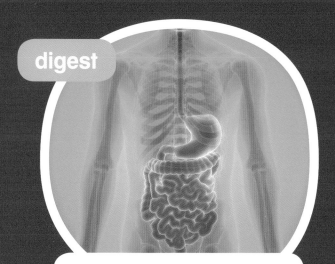

to break down food to be used for energy

fiber

the part of plant foods that the body cannot break down

mineral

a nutrient such as iron, zinc, and others that your body needs for good health

vitamin

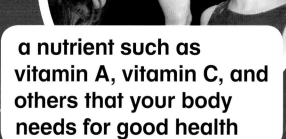

a nutrient such as vitamin A, vitamin C, and others that your body needs for good health

23

Read More

Black, Vanessa. *Fruits*. Minneapolis: Jump!, 2017.

Hoffmann, Sara E. *Kinds of Fruits*. Minneapolis: LernerClassroom, 2013.

Reinke, Beth Bence, MS, RD. *Why We Eat Grains*. Minneapolis: Lerner Publications, 2019.

Index

Photo Credits